Contents

T0346376

Written by
Dennis Hamley
and **David Grant**

Illustrated by
Mark Boardman

Series editor **Dee Reid**

Heinemann

Part of Pearson

Characters

Ryan

The Girl

Tricky words

- caught
- accelerated
- remember
- voice
- skeleton
- exactly
- accident
- vanished

Read these words to the student. Help them with these words when they appear in the text.

Introduction

Ryan stole cars for the thrill of it. He liked to nick smart old cars because they were easy to break into. He was never caught. One night Ryan spotted an Aston Martin. The door was unlocked. The keys were there as if they were waiting for him. Ryan drove off and accelerated to 100mph.

Revenge

Ryan stole cars for the thrill of it.
He liked to nick smart old cars
because they were easy to break into.
When Ryan saw the right kind of car
he would break in and then drive off.
He was never caught.

One night Ryan was out again,
looking for a car to break into.
He came to a road with big
houses on both sides.
Ryan had been here before.

Ryan spotted an old Aston Martin by one of the big houses. He had stolen one just like it about a year ago.

He tried the door. It was unlocked.
The keys were there as if they were waiting for him.
Amazing!
Ryan got in and sank into the soft seats.

He started the engine and drove off as fast as he could. He saw no police cars, so he accelerated up to 100mph.

"Do you remember last year?" said a voice.
Ryan jumped. Who said that?

"Very soon now," said the voice.
There was a girl sitting beside him.
She was young and pretty.
Her face was pale in the moonlight.
Where had she come from?

Ryan was sure that the car had been
empty when he got in.
So how come there was a girl sitting next to him?
Ryan was really worried. He hoped she wouldn't
get him into trouble for nicking the car.

"Very soon now," she said again.
Ryan looked at her.
He knew he'd seen her before but
he couldn't remember where.

She turned towards him.
She was pretty, but there was something
strange about her. Her face was very white
and her lips were very red. She had very dark
eyes which burned into him.

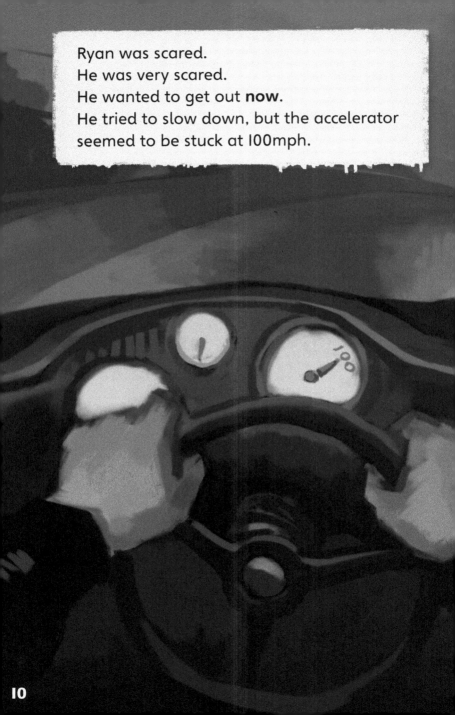

Ryan was scared.
He was very scared.
He wanted to get out **now**.
He tried to slow down, but the accelerator
seemed to be stuck at 100mph.

"This is it," said the girl.
She gripped his arm like a vice.

He looked down.
The hand on his arm wasn't the
hand of a girl.
It was the bony hand of a skeleton!

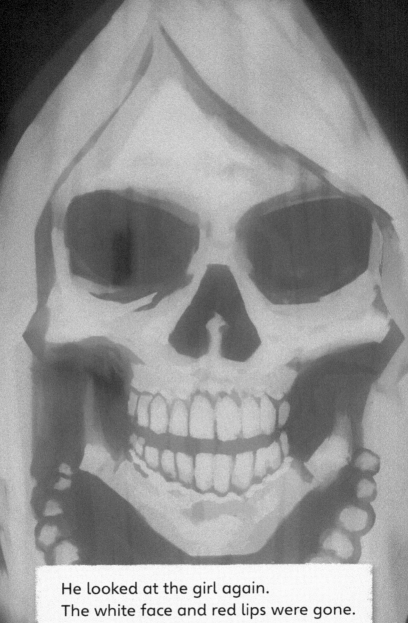

He looked at the girl again.
The white face and red lips were gone.
Now he saw a skull.
He wanted to scream.

The lights ahead turned red.
Now he remembered.
It wasn't **about** a year ago that he stole the Aston Martin.
It was EXACTLY a year ago.

The same car.
The same road.
The same red lights.
The same girl!

Ryan hadn't stopped at the red light.
He hadn't seen the girl in the road until
it was too late.
He hadn't stopped at the scene of the accident.
Nobody knew who the hit-and-run driver was.

GIRL KILLED IN HIT-AND-RUN ACCIDENT

The bony fingers pulled at his arm.
There was a big tree ahead.
He tried to turn the steering wheel,
but the girl's fingers were too strong.

The Aston Martin smashed into the tree.
The girl stepped out of the smashed
car and smiled. Then she vanished.
Poor old Ryan.
If only he had stopped at the red light.

Literal comprehension
p3 Why did Ryan choose smart old cars to nick?
p10 Why doesn't Ryan slow down?

Inferential comprehension
p5 Why were the keys in the Aston Martin?
p7 What does the girl mean when she says 'Very soon now'?
p16 What has happened to Ryan?

Personal response
- When did you begin to suspect things would go wrong for Ryan?
- Do you think Ryan deserves what happens to him?

Word knowledge
p11 What simile is used on this page?
p13 Why is the word 'exactly' in capital letters?
p16 Find a word that means 'disappeared'.

Spelling challenge

Read these words:
because   wanted   lovely
Now try to spell them!

Ha! Ha! Ha!

Why did the ghost not go to the party?

Because he had no body to go with!

Find out about

- car theft and how it might be stopped.

Tricky words

- thieves
- expensive
- documents
- arrested
- easiest
- vehicle
- Bahamas
- instruction

Read these words to the student. Help them with these words when they appear in the text.

Introduction

Car crime is a big problem in Britain. Thieves steal nearly 150,000 cars a year. Some car thieves work in gangs. They steal expensive cars and then make new number plates and documents for the cars. Then they sell them. Some thieves steal boats and planes as well!

CAR CRIME

Car crime is a big problem.
Sometimes thieves steal a car and
then sell it.
Nearly 150,000 cars are stolen in
Britain every year.

Sometimes thieves break into cars and
steal something from the car.
Nearly half of the drivers in Britain
have either had their car stolen or had
something stolen from their car.

Expensive cars

In 2010, 14 members of a gang were sent to prison for stealing cars. The gang looked for houses with expensive cars parked outside. They would break into the house and steal the car keys.

They gave the cars new number plates and made new documents for the cars.

Then they sold them.

None of the people who bought the cars knew that they were stolen.

When the thieves were arrested,
the police found £100,000 in cash
in one of their houses.
The police think that the gang stole
and then sold cars worth about
£4 million in total!

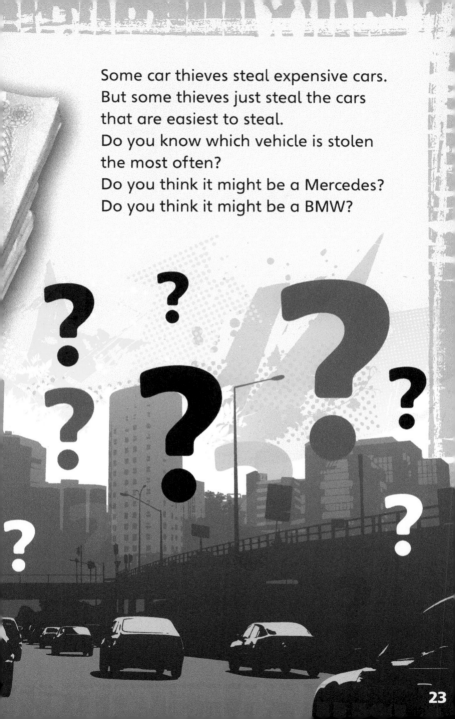

Some car thieves steal expensive cars. But some thieves just steal the cars that are easiest to steal.

Do you know which vehicle is stolen the most often?

Do you think it might be a Mercedes?

Do you think it might be a BMW?

No.
The Transit Van is the vehicle that is stolen most often!
Maybe thieves think there will be something worth stealing in the back of the van.

Barefoot Bandit

Thieves don't just steal cars.
A thief in America was arrested in 2010
for stealing cars, boats and planes.
He was known as the Barefoot Bandit
because he did lots of his crimes
without any shoes on.

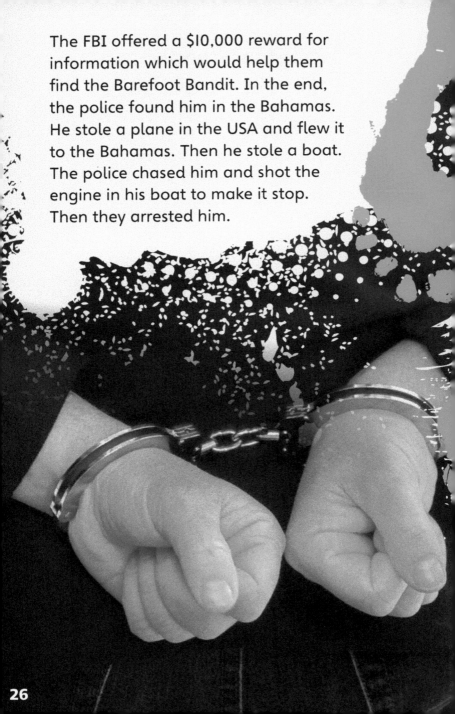

The FBI offered a $10,000 reward for information which would help them find the Barefoot Bandit. In the end, the police found him in the Bahamas. He stole a plane in the USA and flew it to the Bahamas. Then he stole a boat. The police chased him and shot the engine in his boat to make it stop. Then they arrested him.

The Barefoot Bandit was just 19 years old. The police think he learnt how to fly planes by reading plane instruction books and by playing flying games on his computer.

The Barefoot Bandit was not all bad.
Just before he was arrested,
he left $100 on the desk at a vet's.
He also left a note.
The note said: 'Drove by, had some extra cash.
Please use this money for the care of animals'.

Drove by, had some extra cash. Please use this money for the care of animals.

Stop thief!

Soon you will be able to find out if someone is stealing your car just by looking at your mobile phone.
If thieves break into your car, the computer in your car will send a message to your phone.

Your phone will show you a
map which tells you where the
thieves are driving your car.
You can then phone 999 and tell
the police.
Then you can press a key on your
phone and stop the car's engine.

If you put a small camera in the car you'll even be able to see the thieves while they steal your car – and while they are arrested!
Maybe that will be the end of car theft.

Literal comprehension

p24 What vehicle is stolen most often?

p25 Why was the thief called the Barefoot Bandit?

Inferential comprehension

p26 How do you know the FBI really wanted to catch the Barefoot Bandit?

p28 Why did the Barefoot Bandit leave money at the vet's?

p30 How will new technology help stop car crime?

Personal response

- Do you think technology will stop car crime?
- Do you think the Barefoot Bandit was brave or reckless?

Word knowledge

p19 Find two plurals on this page.

p22 Find a word that means 'discovered'.

p23 Find an adjective on this page.

Spelling challenge

Read these words:

sometimes   none   great

Now try to spell them!

Ha! Ha! Ha!

What streets do ghosts haunt?

Dead ends!

32